The Ultimate Interview Quiz!

101 Things Hiring Managers Need to Know

Dawn Moss MCIPD

Interviewing the best people requires the best interviewers!

First Published in 2014
Printed and bound by Amazon createspace
Designed by Pixel Studios: http://www.fiverr.com/pixelstudio
This book is printed on demand so no copies will be remaindered or
pulped – responsible printing.

ISBN-13 9781499171778
ISBN-10 1499171773

How much do you really know about effective recruitment and UK Employment Law?

Reduce your legal, financial and reputational risks with this handy quick quiz.

Are you ready to take the interview self assessment?

Contents

Introduction

Introduction

Hiring the right people, with the right skills at the right time for your business is one of the most critical activities you will undertake – even getting it right first time will cost money but getting it wrong will cost you significantly more financially, legally and potentially damage your hard earned business reputation.

I've been interviewing for many years and supported hundreds of managers through the recruitment process. I've also worked outside of HR and know what it's like managing people and hiring for my own team.

The Quiz

This informative quiz was designed as a prerequisite to my **Interview Guide & Toolkit** and a self assessment.

The quiz is presented in the same format as the Interview Guide and takes you through the entire recruitment process from start to finish and onwards to ensuring a smooth on-boarding process.

How this Interview Self Assessment is Structured.

Each Section relates to each step in the recruitment process and if you purchase the toolkit it mirrors the Chapters of the Interview Guide.

We all have our own preferences for learning – if you're a little impatient like me and like skipping to the end then this is ideal as you can see how much you know before having to read the whole guide.

So this gives you an ideal sneak peek into the content of the toolkit and an opportunity to test your current knowledge before purchasing the whole kit.

The Interview Guide & Toolkit

The Interview Guide for busy Managers will make the whole process very simple to understand and walk you through step by step.

Employment Law can feel like a minefield and for that reason I've given lots of examples, case studies, templates and do's and don'ts.

> *"Knowing is not enough, we must apply.
> Willingness is not enough, we must do."*
>
> **Johann Wolfgang von Goethe**

We hope you enjoy the quiz and learn lots!

Interview Guide for Busy Managers is available at the following address: http://www.yourinterviewcoach.co.uk

Quiz ONE

The Recruitment Process

The fundamental and ultimate purpose of the recruitment process is to find the right people, with the right skills at the right time and more important these days at the right price!

Everything in-between is about getting the process right.

Let's not make the process more complicated than it needs to be. Firstly, you define the requirements of the job, then decide where you are going to advertise to find these people with the skills and knowledge and then you have a robust selection process to ensure you offer the job to the right person. The end!

Okay there's a bit more to share but you get my point. Yes it's a critical process to the successful operation of your business and no one knows this more than me and I'm continuously surprised that this process doesn't get more dedicated attention than it does.

Importance of an Effective Recruitment & Selection Process

There are many factors impacting best practice Recruitment and Selection. Recruiting a new hire can be very costly and take up valuable management time, for this reason, it's important to get it right first time!

You are likely to want to focus your attentions and time on your core business and developing new business – the recruitment process is often an interruption to your day job or core business activities!

- Recruiting the right people is probably the most critical determinant in an organisation's short, medium and long term success.

- Recruitment is expensive and costly

- Recruitment is time consuming

- Recruitment is labour intensive

- Recruitment is largely unscientific (You say "Art" - I say "Science" – let's call the whole thing off!)

The Recruitment Process ~ Quiz One

Questions

1. What are the six main steps in a typical recruitment process from start to finish?
2. Name at least four important factors to consider for an effective recruitment process?
3. What other factors impact the recruitment process?
4. Name at least three of the most common selection problems?
5. Name at least another three common sourcing and selection problems?
6. How would you solve or overcome these sourcing and selection problems?
7. Explain the different types of costs relating to the recruitment process if you get it right first time?
8. Explain the different types of costs relating to ineffective recruitment?
9. How can poor recruitment impact the business?
10. What other consequences are there with managing the recruitment process poorly?

Notes:

_____

_____

_____

_____

_____

_____

_____

_____

_____

Quiz TWO

How much do you know about UK Employment Law?

The recruitment process, more than perhaps any other stage of the employment relationship, engages almost the full range of employment law issues such as discrimination because of Age, Disability, Gender Reassignment, Marriage and civil partnership, Pregnancy & Maternity, Race, Religion or belief, Sex and / or Sexual Orientation.

The Recruitment process (job description, advertising, screening CVs, conducting interviews, conducting and making offers) is also concerned with aspects of data protection, immigration, human rights (pre-employment checks, the use of medical testing and inquiries about criminal history) the law concerning contracts, and statutory employment rights.

Employment Law is complicated – there's no denying it. However, if you stick to the script – meaning if you only think about the skills, knowledge and types of experience required you will naturally reduce the risk of getting into trouble.

Also if you have a well thought out process – rather than trying to "wing it" then you'll get much more information and data to make a good decision a great and well informed decision.

UK Employment Law ~ Quiz Two

Questions

11. When did the Equality Act come into force in the UK?

12. Why was the Equality Act introduced?

13. What are protective characteristics?

14. Name the nine protective characteristics?

15. Name the different types of discrimination?

16. Explain and describe at least two types of discrimination?

17. Where can discrimination happen other than the workplace?

18. What are the three main Employment Tribunals called?

19. Read **case study one** below and answer this question: Does David's decision comply with UK Employment Law? Is this discrimination?

Case Study One

David is a senior manager – he rejects Vicky's application for promotion to a Team Leader role.

Vicky, who is a lesbian, finds out that David did this because he believes the department that she applied to work as a Team Leader is homophobic.

David thought he should try to protect Vicky because her sexual orientation would prevent her from gaining the team's respect and managing them effectively.

---

20. Read **case study two** below and then answer this question: Does this behaviour comply with UK Employment Law? Explain?

Case Study Two

Susan works as a Business Analyst and is looking forward to a promised promotion.

Shortly after the promised offer of a promotion Susan's mother (who lives at her home) had a heart attack. The promotion was then withdrawn.

21. Read **case study three** below and then answer this question: Is this a fair decision to take against Andy? Is this unlawful discrimination?

Case study three

Andy is 45 but looks much younger. Lots of people think that he is in his mid 20s.

It was decided that he would not be allowed to represent his company at an important meeting because the Managing Director thinks that he is too young.

22. Explain the meaning and definition of discrimination by association?

23. Explain the meaning and definition of perceptive discrimination?

24. Is it lawful to ask the following questions?

>   How old are you?
>
>   What is your date of birth?
>
>   Are you married?
>
>   How many children do you have?
>
>   Where are you from originally?
>
>   As there is some travelling associated with this job, how will you manage child care?

25. Is it lawful to include "Five years' experience within a Credit Analysis role is essential" on a job description?

26. Is it lawful to include "Must have at least five GCSEs" on a job description?

27. Is this lawful to include "Part time vacancy – would suit female returning to work" on a job advert?

Notes:

_____

_____

_____

_____

_____

_____

_____

_____

Quiz THREE

How important is the Job Description?

The Job Description ("JD") is the most critical document in the entire process and will to a certain extent determine the success of the hire. The stage before creating an accurate job description and person specification is the job analysis.

Job Analysis Methods

Job Analysis can be a time consuming and an in-depth process and there are many ways of conducting the initial job analysis. The most reliable and convenient method is to ask those people already doing the job – although if it's a new position you'll need to do some research before putting together an accurate and concise job description.

Job Description

Getting the job description and person specification right is the first step in the recruitment process and will then lead into writing accurate adverts, selecting the right candidates for interview and asking the right questions to gather information and data on the person's future capability, ability and competence. This is an important point – so please read again!

The Job Description ~ Quiz Three

Questions

28. Name two methods of conducting a job analysis?

29. Name at least three reasons why getting the job description accurate is critical to the success of the recruitment process?

30. Describe the differences between the job description and the person specification?

31. Name at least four elements that should be included on the job description or person specification?

32. Explain the reasons for not including length of experience in a job description?

Notes:

_____

_____

_____

_____

_____

_____

_____

_____

Quiz FOUR

Sourcing Methods
Do you know where to attract & find the right People?

Sourcing basically means where you will find the best candidates to match the job.

Where are you going to advertise to attract relevant candidates?

Where are you going to find the most appropriate and relevant candidates?

Where would these candidates normally look, search and apply for jobs?

Where do these people hang out!! Candidate attraction is finding the most appropriate and the best talent for your business.

Sourcing Methods ~ Quiz Four

Questions

33. Name at least four different methods of sourcing (finding and attracting candidates)?

34. Name at least four essential items that should be included in an external advert for it to be effective?

35. Find out two specialist publications, journals or job boards relating to your industry?

36. Describe the difference between Contingency Terms and Executive Search when using a Recruitment Agency?

37. Name at least two ways to attract candidates without costing any money?

38. Name at least four ways to reduce the recruitment spend?

39. Is it lawful to include the following words in a job advert – Energetic or Dynamic?

40. Is it lawful to include "This vacancy would suit female returning to work" in a job advert?

41. Is it lawful to include "We are looking for professional and mature candidates'" in a job advert?

Notes:

_____

_____

_____

_____

_____

_____

_____

_____

Quiz FIVE

**Selection Methods
Are you getting the best
information during the
interview to Assess
People's Skills and
Capability?**

What are selection methods? This is the time to use certain tools or techniques to assess the candidate's ability to perform in the job.

What tools are you going to use to select the best candidate for the job? There are so many methods to choose from however here in the UK the interview is the most used vehicle to making a decision about a candidate.

I get really excited about the different methods available to hiring managers – I know it's sad but I'm still a recruiter at heart! It's just a shame these different and varied methods are not fully utilised.

Don't misunderstand me – I'm a big advocate for the good old fashion structured interview. I'm an even bigger fan of the **Behavioural Competency** style interview and have been using this method with success for over a decade.

No it's not a new method but it's traditional, tried and tested! More importantly if you know how to fully apply this knowledge it really works.

Worth mentioning at this point is validity and reliability – whatever selection method you decide to use it must be relevant to the job role and assess the skills and knowledge required by the incumbent.

Selection Methods ~ Quiz Five

Questions

42. Name at least four different methods of selection?

43. What are the key items to screen on a CV?

44. Name at least three different types of interview?

45. What does reliability and validity mean?

46. Name two hard skills and two soft skills?

47. Name two different types of motivational fit?

48. Write at least four questions to assess a candidate's motivation?

49. Explain the possible risks associated with changing the job criteria half way throughout the recruitment process?

50. Explain what you would need to do if you were to change the job requirements half way through the recruitment process?

Notes:

_____

_____

_____

_____

_____

_____

_____

_____

Quiz SIX

How much do you know about the most effective Questioning Techniques?

There are many different types of questions however some are more effective for use during job interviews. Think carefully at the planning stage what you want to achieve during the interview. Leave grilling and interrogating to the detectives!

If you're a manager and you've been interviewing for many years you've probably got your faithful stock questions – STOP! Have you asked yourself are these questions really helping you to qualify a candidate's capability? After all that is the main purpose of an interview right!

If you ask these questions to the "polished" "prepared" candidates they'll get out the PowerPoint Presentation, the laser pointer and talk you through the readymade text book answers.

Here's one I made up earlier! Wouldn't you rather get to know the real person? The real person that you will be working with Monday to Friday 9am to 5pm! You need to understand if they are capable of doing the job they are being employed to do. Therefore, you'll need effective questioning techniques.

Questioning Techniques ~ Quiz Six

Questions

51. If you decide to design an assessment centre name at least three exercises?

52. If an internal candidate undertook a psychometric ability test 18 months ago, would this information still be usable to make decisions?

53. Can you use personality questionnaires as part of a screening in and out exercise?

54. Can you use an accuracy test to screen in and out candidates from the recruitment process?

55. What would you do if a candidate undertaking a psychometric test informs you that they have dyslexia?

56. Can psychometric tests be stored in personnel files?

57. Name at least four different types of questions?

58. Describe the disadvantages of asking hypothetical questions during the interview?

59. Describe the pros and cons of asking closed questions?

60. Exercise: Decide if these questions are behavioural, theoretical /hypothetical, opinion or leading?

- How would you usually handle difficult people?

- Why did you decide to do that?

- Tell me how you learnt that skill?

- You say their processes were inefficient – how would you change them?

- What would your ideal job be?

- Are you a good team player?

Notes:

_____

_____

_____

_____

_____

_____

_____

_____

Quiz SEVEN

What are Behavioural Competencies and how do you use them to good effect during the interview process?

What are behavioural competencies?

There are several definitions to consider. Generally it's about demonstrating the ability to perform a specific role.

"A competence is a standardised and measurable requirement for an individual to correctly perform a specific job. It is a combination of knowledge, skills and behaviour which may be utilised to improve performance."

During the interview you are attempting to predict the future behaviour and capability of that candidate in the job role and the best method to be able to do this with as much certainty as possible is by gathering evidence from that candidate's past using the Behavioural Competency Style Questions.

If you believe the research on Predictive Validity then you'll understand that the more structured the interview and the more relevant information you gather during the interview then the more likely you are to get closer to selecting the best fitting candidate. If you rely on a CV or just having an informal "chat" with a candidate then it's more likely going to decrease the chance of getting the right fit.

Behavioural Competencies ~ Quiz Seven

Questions

61. Why do we use behavioural competencies to assess candidates during interview?

62. Name at least four different behavioural competencies?

63. What does the acronym S.T.A.R. stand for?

64. Name four key words to watch during the interview?

Notes:

Quiz EIGHT

What's involved in planning the interview?

Spending time carefully planning the interview itself, is time well spent. If you don't you could lose valuable time thinking on your feet and trying to come up with the questions during a conversation.

To ensure you maximise your time during the interview, it is essential to carefully plan what you are going to cover at each stage.

If you don't have a set of standard questions you may forget to ask all candidates the same questions. This could lead to one candidate getting more opportunities to demonstrate skills and knowledge putting others at a disadvantage.

If you don't review the CV properly and write down the specific background questions you have, again you could waste valuable time or forget important fact finding questions to clarify vague or missing information or gaps in their career history.

If you don't prepare, then the candidate is likely to control the interview and can control the information they share. We can pretty much guarantee that the candidate will only share positive information. If you don't prepare, then you are likely to base decisions on feelings or impressions during the interview rather than objective criteria.

Planning the Interview ~ Quiz Eight

Questions

65. Name at least five things you should consider when planning an interview?

66. Name at least four different agenda items to cover during a typical interview?

67. What could happen if you don't review the CV properly or plan the CV background questions?

68. Can you complete the introductions and talk through the format of the interview in 120 seconds?

Notes:

_____

_____

_____

_____

_____

_____

_____

Quiz NINE

Are there rules when Observing & Recording Data during the interview?

During the interview itself there are a number of activities being performed by the interviewer. You are attempting to build rapport with the candidate (trying to avoid asking any questions that will get you into trouble!), concentrating on the information being shared and asking appropriate follow up / probing questions to gather more information and clarify.

You are also (whether you know it or not!) subconsciously picking up hundreds of pieces of data (body language, subtle signals, tone of voice, gestures, facial expressions and many other pieces of information.)

It is recommended that you do not try to assess or judge the information you are gathering because there is so much going on during the interaction between you and the candidate.

Don't make up your mind during the interview about the suitability of this person for the job until you've completed the whole process and then give yourself time after the interview to review the information.

Okay, this is not as easy as it sounds – most of us make very quick decisions on people within the first few minutes – some in seconds!! The way someone is dressed, their accent, the way they communicate and present themselves, if the person has tattoos or piercings – we've already made up our minds about what that person is like! This is crazy!

Not only could you be missing out on a good candidate, you could be allowing your own bias or prejudice to get in the way of assessing objectively.

At the extreme you could be increasing your risk of discrimination if you cannot document your decision making process objectively and against the job criteria.

Trust me (I'm an in-house recruiter!!) an employment tribunal judge will not be impressed if you say the decision was based on gut feelings.

Observation & Recording Information ~ Quiz Nine

Questions

69. Give four reasons why taking notes is important?

70. What is "active listening"?

71. Describe why active listening is important during the interview process?

72. What are you trying not to do during the interview?

73. Give four tips on "active listening"?

74. How would you ensure you understood the information being shared during the interview? What techniques would you use?

75. If you take lots of notes and don't maintain eye contact what are you in danger of doing?

76. For what period of time should you keep notes and records on unsuccessful candidates?

Notes:

_____

_____

_____

_____

_____

_____

_____

_____

Quiz TEN

Assessment & Evaluation

Evaluation takes place immediately after the interview and involves reviewing the information and data gathered during the interview. It's best to review that day or you'll forget the subtleties associated with the interview.

Even if you've taken really good notes (which we highly recommend), you'll easily lose some of the meanings behind the words.

Most of us will know that verbal communication is only part of what we observe during the interview – we are also taking in body language, tone of voice, facial expressions.

Body Language accounts for 55%
Tone of Voice accounts for 38%
Spoken Word accounts for 7%

The behavioural indicators of the skills presented act as your guide for evaluating the effectiveness of the behaviour that you have observed and recorded. The indicators are lists of typical behaviours that you might expect to see in both high performing and low performing candidates. These are in the format of positive and negative indicators.

Firstly, you and your interviewing partner should go through the interview notes highlight the key positive and negative behavioural examples. During the interview you have been acting simply as a collector and recorder of what you have seen and heard. Next you should tick those behavioural indicators that the individual has demonstrated and which are covered in your notes.

Your record of the interview must be an adequate description of the candidate's behaviour, and should be supported by examples. Similarly do not give your judgements of the candidate's behaviour without some supporting description. Words such as "good" and "bad" are judgemental rather than descriptive, and in absence of behavioural evidence, they fail to give any clues about why the candidates were good or bad.

Assessment & Evaluation ~ Quiz Ten

Questions

77. What is a Subject Access Request?

78. Why should you *not* write down your opinion during the interview?

79. When should you evaluate and assess information gathered on the candidates?

80. What percentage of communication is body language?

81. What do you need to have with every behavioural competency in order to measure a candidate's competence and future ability?

82. What percentage of communication is the spoken word?

83. Explain the horns effect in recruitment terms?

84. Explain the halo effect in recruitment terms?

Notes:

_____

_____

_____

_____

_____

_____

_____

_____

Quiz ELEVEN

Do you know what's involved in the Offer Stage & what about the Background Checks?

It's time to make an offer and carry out the all important necessary background checks.

Both stages need to be carefully managed, although, some of the work to ensure this stage runs smoothly should have been done throughout the recruitment process.

Candidates who have made it to the final stages of the recruitment process should fully understand the organisation, the job requirements and be engaged and want to join your business.

All that hard work, advertising, screening hundreds of CVs and interviewing candidates is paid back as we approach the chosen one!

Offer Stage & Background Checks ~ Quiz Eleven

Questions

85. What are the two main types of offers of employment?

86. Name the two strands of a conditional offer of employment?

87. How long do you have after someone starts working to issue a written contract?

88. What should be included in a formal offer letter?

89. What are the minimum requirements by law to include in a contract of employment?

90. Name the three main background check categories?

91. Name four items included in a typical background check?

92. What nationalities are automatically eligible to work in the UK?

93. Is a verbal offer a legally binding contract in the UK?

94. What is the Disclosure and Barring Service and what did it replace?

Notes:

_____

_____

_____

_____

_____

_____

_____

_____

Quiz TWELVE

How much is involved in the Induction & On-boarding process?

Welcome aboard! This is where you can really stand out from the crowd! We've talked mostly about **you** making the right decision – but it's just as much the candidates decision to join your business and here they are on their first day.

On-boarding is the process of bringing a new employee to the organisation and providing information, training, mentoring and coaching throughout the transition.

It's time to continue the good work you've done managing the relationship throughout the recruitment process and give your new starter a warm welcome. Remember we mentioned the importance of the psychological contract and how this starts when you first advertise this is an important stage in the employment relationship to show how much you value your new joiner and welcome them to the organisation.

Bearing in mind I've been a new starter a few times now – I've experienced some far from satisfactory first days! Dirty desks, no PC, or telephone – rubbish in the drawers left over from my predecessor and don't get me started on the state of the keyboards!

Induction & On-boarding Process ~ Quiz Twelve

Questions

95. Name five items to cover with a new joiner on their first day?

96. Name at least two items relating to the company orientation and induction?

97. Name two items relating to the job orientation and induction?

98. Name two items an employer believes is an implied condition of the psychological contract

99. Name two items an employee believes is an implied condition of the psychological contract?

100. What are the possible risks once a candidate has handed in their notice?

101. What should you do to mitigate the possible risks once the candidate has handed in their notice?

Notes:

_____

_____

_____

_____

_____

_____

_____

_____

_____

FINISHED!

How confident are you?

How many questions do you think you've got right?

Time to check your answers!!

CONCLUSION

Hiring the right people, with the right skills at the right time for your business is one of the most critical activities you will undertake – even getting it right first time will cost money but getting it wrong will cost you significantly more financially, legally and potentially damage the businesses reputation.

Having supported hundreds of managers to source and select the best talent for their business sectors, I know how important it is to spend quality time planning the process from start to finish.

The ultimate purpose and aim of the recruitment process is to attract and retain the most suitable candidates that match the organisation, the culture and the job role. If you can go through this process fairly, consistently, objectively and manage the people positively regardless of the outcome then you have succeeded. When you receive good feedback from candidates that have been rejected then you really know you've followed a clear and transparent process.

In my experience prevention is better than cure with any activity relating to Human Resource Management.

Getting the process right for your business and being compliant with the latest legislation makes good business sense financially and legally.

It's cliché but people are your best asset and probably your biggest expense too, so getting it right first time is critical.

Spending the time getting it right is definitely time well spent and will achieve a greater return on your investment!

"The price of success is hard work, dedication to the job at hand, and determination that whether we win or lose we have applied the best of ourselves to the task at hand."

Vince Lombardi

THE
ANSWERS!

Recruitment Process ~ Quiz One Answers

1. What are the six main steps in a typical recruitment process from start to finish?

   - Conducting the Job Analysis
   - Creating the Job Description (often the process starts here)
   - Sourcing the candidates
   - CV screening and short-listing
   - Selecting the candidates
   - Offer Negotiation

2. Name at least four important factors to consider for an effective recruitment process?

   - Accurate job description
   - Accurate screening criteria to effectively select candidates that best match
   - Valid and reliable selection methods
   - Excellent questioning techniques to select the best talent

3. What other factors impact the recruitment process?

- Morale of existing team
- Turnover – too high or too low. Aim to get a healthy balance of stability and new ideas.
- Consider the reputation of the organisation when you start communicating to candidates
- Remember the learning curve and any training and development time in the role before the new hire is fully productive in the role

4. Name at least three of the most common selection problems?

- Asking illegal, unlawful, non job related questions – increasing the risk of Employment Tribunal claims (Legal, Financial & Reputational Damage)
- Poor screening of candidates CVs
- Interviewers overlook job motivation and cultural fit

5. Name at least another three common selection problems?

- Putting candidates off the organisation – reputational damage is difficult to calculate the costs or loss of clients
- Letting bias affect judgement (stereotyping, halo/horns, generalisations)
- Interviewers miss important information or evidence
- Insufficient notes

6. How would you solve or overcome these selection problems?

Ask yourself these questions:
- Has the selection process been fair?
- Has the sourcing and selection process been objective?
- Have all the candidates been treated consistently?
- Have the methods been appropriate for the job?
- Have the right questions been asked?
- Has the process been robust, valid and reliable?

7. Explain the different types of costs relating to the recruitment process if you get it right first time?

- Advertising costs
- Recruitment Agency costs and placement fees
- Management Time – Screening CVs, time spent interviewing etc.
- Time it takes to hire – empty seat. Calculate lost revenue or sales
- Costs associated with the learning curve, training and development time

8. Explain the different types of costs relating to ineffective recruitment?

- Employment Tribunal costs
- Legal costs associated with hiring a specialist employment lawyer

9. How can poor recruitment impact the business?

- Morale of team
- Productivity
- Learning curve and the time it takes new joiners to get up to speed
- Time for training and development

10. What other consequences are there with managing the recruitment process poorly?

- Negative or bad press or negative word of mouth if candidates are being treated poorly
- Damage to business reputation
- Increased risk of Employment Tribunal costs
- Increase risk of discrimination claims if the business doesn't follow a process

82

UK Employment Law ~ Quiz Two Answers

11. When did the Equality Act come into force in the UK?

   - Equality Act 2010 – came into force on October 1st 2010

12. Why was the Equality Act introduced?

   - Consolidates nine separate pieces of anti-discrimination legislation into a single act and updates and amends existing strands of anti-discrimination law, but does not completely re-codify it – so differences between the different strands remain.

13. What are protective characteristics?

   - The concept behind the nine protected characteristics makes it unlawful to discriminate or make decisions based on these particular personal characteristics – see list below.

14. Name the nine protective characteristics?

- Age
- Disability
- Gender Re-Assignment
- Marriage & Civil Partnership
- Pregnancy & Maternity
- Race
- Religion or Belief
- Sex
- Sexual Orientation

15. Name the different types of discrimination?

- Direct discrimination
- Associative discrimination
- Perceptive discrimination
- Indirect discrimination
- Harassment
- Victimisation

16. Explain and describe at least two types of discrimination?

- "Direct discrimination occurs when someone is treated less favourably than another person because of a protected characteristic they have or are thought to have (see perception discrimination below), or because they are associated with someone who has a protected characteristic."

17. Where can discrimination happen other than the workplace?

- Education
- as a consumer
- when using public services
- when buying or renting property
- as a member or guest of a private club or association

18. What are the three main Employment Tribunals called?

- Employment Tribunal ET
- Employment Appeals Tribunal EAT
- Court of Appeal

Case Study One

David is a senior manager – he rejects Vicky's application for promotion to a Team Leader role.

Vicky, who is a lesbian, finds out that David did this because he believes the department that she applied to work as a Team Leader is homophobic.

David thought he should try to protect Vicky because her sexual orientation would prevent her from gaining the team's respect and managing them effectively.

19. Does David's decision comply with UK Employment Law? No. Is this discrimination? Yes.

   - Note: This **does** **not** comply with employment law. This is **direct discrimination** because of Vicky's sexual orientation.

Case Study Two
Susan works as a Business Analyst and is looking forward to a promised promotion.   Shortly after the promised offer of a promotion Susan's mother (who lives at her home) had a heart attack.   The promotion was then withdrawn.

20. Does this behaviour comply with UK Employment Law? No. Explain? Yes.

- Note: This **does not** comply with employment law. This may be **associative discrimination** against Susan because of her association with a disabled person.

Case study three

Andy is 45 but looks much younger. Lots of people think that he is in his mid 20s.

It was decided that he would not be allowed to represent his company at an important meeting because the Managing Director thinks that he is too young.

21. Is this fair? Is this unlawful discrimination?

- Andy has been discriminated against on the perception of a protected characteristic i.e. Age

22. Explain the meaning and definition of discrimination by association?

- "Discrimination by association occurs when a person is treated less favourably because they are linked or associated with a protected characteristic. The person does not have the protected characteristic but they are treated less favourably than others because of a protected characteristic of a friend, spouse, partner, parent or another person with whom they are associated."

23. Explain the meaning and definition of perceptive discrimination?

- "Discrimination by perception happens when a person is discriminated against because they are thought to have a particular protected characteristic when in fact they do not. If you discriminate against people because you think they are transsexual or gay, for example, then they will be protected even if they do not have these protected characteristics."

24. Is it lawful to ask the following questions?

- How old are you? No
- What is your date of birth? No
- Are you married? No
- How many children do you have? No
- Where are you from originally? No
- As there is some travelling associated with this job, how will you manage child care? No

All of these questions are unlawful or illegal under the Equality Act 2010.

25. Is it lawful to include "Five years experience within a Credit Analysis role is essential" on a job description?

- This is illegal under the Equality Act 2010 (Relates to Age Discrimination.) The length of experience requirements are now viewed as potentially discriminatory in respect of Age Discrimination.

26. Is it lawful to include "Must have at least five GCSE's" on a job description?

- This is illegal under the Equality Act 2010 Age Discrimination – Qualification requirements. Think carefully about any qualification listed under the qualifications and training section of the JD. Are they really required?

27. Is this lawful to include "Part time vacancy – would suit female returning to work" on a job advert?

- This is illegal under the Equality Act 2010 Sex Discrimination. If you advertised for a particularly gender this would be direct discrimination. In recruitment you must not assume that part time work would only suit a female and should welcome all applications.

Job Description ~ Quiz Three Answers

28. Name two methods of conducting a job analysis?

- Diaries
- Interviews
- Observations
- Repertory grids
- Checklists & Inventories

29. Name at least three reasons why getting the job description accurate is critical to the success of the recruitment process?

- Advertising Campaigns
- Candidate Attraction
- CV Screening Criteria
- Selection Methods - Valid & Reliable
- Questioning Techniques

30. Describe the differences between the job description and the person specification?

- The Job Description outlines the tasks and duties – what the person can expect to do in the role and what tasks and duties will be involved. The Person Specification describes the skills, knowledge and behaviours needed to perform the duties and tasks.

31. Name at least four elements that should be included on the job description or person specification?

- Job Responsibilities - Duties & Tasks, Accountabilities & Responsibilities, Job Content etc
- Person Specification – Essential & Desirable (skills, knowledge, qualifications.)
- Behavioural Competencies – five or six should be sufficient
- Technical Competencies (job related skill requirements)
- Key Performance Indicators
- Compliance, regulation or legislation relating to this role
- Relationships – clients and internal customers, suppliers, other departments, divisions and provides, agents etc.

32. Explain the reasons for not including length of experience in a job description?

- Don't state the years of experience. Avoid specifying maximum or minimum lengths of experience. This may be direct discrimination because of Age if you state a requirement of this nature.

Sourcing Methods ~ Quiz Four Answers

33. Name at least four different methods of sourcing (finding and attracting candidates)?

- Internal advertising
- Employee Referral Schemes
- External advertising
- Social Media
- Recruitment Agencies
- Job Centre Plus (JCP)
- Job Fairs or Open Days
- Networking

34. Name at least four essential items that should be included in an external advert for it to be effective?

- Job title
- Job Tasks & Duties
- Job Criteria – essential and desirable skills, knowledge and type of experience
- Salary
- Location
- Selling points
- Travel requirements

35. Find out two specialist publications, journals or job boards relating to your industry?

- HR – Personnel Today
- Legal – The Lawyer
- Banking & Finance – eFinancial Careers
- IT – IT Job Board
- Grocer – FMCG Experts

36. Describe the difference between Contingency Terms and Executive Search when using a Recruitment Agency?

- If you set up contingency terms this usually means you do not pay the recruitment agency until the successful candidate has commenced employment.
- If you set up terms with an Executive Search Firm you are likely to work exclusively with the agency and by agreement and negotiation potentially pay an upfront non-refundable fee and then 1/3 on receipt of the shortlist of potential candidates and then a 1/3 when identifying the successful candidate. Everything is up for negotiation – after all you are the client!!

37. Name at least two ways to attract candidates without costing any money?

- Jobcentre Plus – advertising on the website is free
- Advertising on your own website is free
- Advertising on most social media platforms are free

38. Name at least four ways to reduce the recruitment spend?

- Employee Referral Scheme
- Negotiate with current third party suppliers
- Advertise on specialist job boards
- Outsource to a Virtual Recruitment Department – it's often more economical to hire the experts to manage the process (quicker and more efficient).

39. Is it lawful to include the following words in a job advert – Energetic or Dynamic?

- It's not unlawful however the use of such words has connotations or perceptions of age. Therefore, it could heighten the risk of claims for Age Discrimination.

40. Is it lawful to include "This vacancy would suit female returning to work" in a job advert?

- No it's not lawful under the Sex Discrimination Act – which is one of the protected characteristics relating to the Equality Act 2010.

41. Is it lawful to include "We are looking for professional and mature candidates'" in a job advert?

- No it's not lawful. The use of the word mature almost certainly implies a candidate of a certain age. Therefore, could increase the risk of Age Discrimination claims.

Selection Methods ~ Quiz Five Answers

42. Name at least four different methods of selection?

- Unstructured Interview
- Panel Interview
- Assessment Centres (Role Plays, Group Exercises, Presentations etc.)
- Telephone Interviews
- Psychometric Tests (Ability Tests & Personality Questionnaires)
- Behavioural Competency Interviews (Structured Interviews)

43. What are the key items to screen on a CV?

- Knowledge & skills (hard & soft skills)
- Types of experience – not length of experience or time span
- Qualifications – as long as these are justified for the position
- Training certificates
- Hints of behavioural evidence:
  - Ability to learn, College or University, other evidence of studying and the grades achieved.

- Client relationships, client management, liaising with clients, managing requirements, delivering a service or solution that you will consider in candidate selection.

44. Name at least three different types of interview?

- Telephone Interview
- Panel Interview
- Assessment Centres
- Unstructured interviews – informal or just a chat
- Behavioural Competency Style interviews

45. What does reliability and validity mean?

- Validity = Valid for the purposes of the competence being measured
- Reliability = Consistency of the measure and produces similar results

46. Name two hard skills and two soft skills?

- Hard skills = IT systems skills, Financial or Accounting skills, Typing skills, Producing Management Information, Analytical skills.
- Soft skills = Related to behaviours such as interpersonal skills, planning and organising skills, communication skills.

47. Name two different types of motivational fit?

- Job Fit
- Corporate Cultural Fit

48. Write at least four questions to assess a candidate's motivation?

- What do you really enjoy in your current job? Which tasks in particular do you like doing?
- What tasks do you find frustrating and would like to do less in the next job role?
- What attracted you to apply and accept the offer of employment at your current/last job?
- What made you select this University to study?
- What is it in particular attracted you to study this subject?

49. Explain the possible risks associated with changing the job criteria half way throughout the recruitment process?

- There may be previously screened and rejected CVs/candidates that may now match the changed criteria.
- This practice could increase the risk of discrimination or you are changing the criteria to fit a particular candidate.

50. Explain what you would need to do if you were to change the job requirements half way through the recruitment process?

- Re-screen all the previous applicants against the new criteria

Questioning Techniques ~ Quiz Six Answers

51. If you decide to design an assessment centre name at least three exercises?

- Role Play
- Group Exercise
- Psychometric Tests
- Presentations

52. If an internal candidate undertook a psychometric ability test 18 months ago, would this information still be usable to make decisions?

- No – psychometric tests have a shelf life of 18 months and must be safely destroyed

53. Can you use personality questionnaires as part of a screening in and out exercise?

- No - personality questionnaires are not intended to be used as part of a screening in and out exercise. Personality questionnaires should not be used in isolation – they should be used as part of the whole process.

54. Can you use an accuracy test to screen in and out candidates from the recruitment process?

- Yes – Ability tests such as the verbal reasoning and numerical tests can be used for volume recruitment to ethically screen out candidates that do not meet the minimum scores

55. What would you do if a candidate undertaking a psychometric test informs you that they have dyslexia?

- Whenever a disability prevents a suitably qualified candidate undergoing a standard selection process - an alternative appropriate method for assessment must be found.

56. Can psychometric tests be stored in personnel files?

- No – best practice means that it is best to store psychometric tests and questionnaire in separate secure cabinets. Only trained and appropriately qualified personnel should have access to previous tests and questionnaires.

57. Name at least four different types of questions?

- Open Questions
- Closed Questions
- Probing or Funnel Questions
- Multiple Questions
- Reflective or Paraphrasing
- Hypothetical / situational Questions
- Leading Questions
- Alternative
- Self assessment

58. Describe the disadvantages of asking hypothetical questions during the interview?

- If you ask a hypothetical question you are likely to get a hypothetical answer. Candidates are likely to talk through a best case scenario or text book answer and we all know working life doesn't happen like a text book!

59. Describe the pros and cons of asking closed questions?

- You are likely to receive a yes or no answer. So there won't be much of a conversation.

- You can ask closed questions before you ask the main questions to check the candidate has had an opportunity to demonstrate that skill or competence. For example, "Have you ever managed staff?" If yes, you can then go on to ask an open / behavioural competency questions. If no, you can use an alternative question to assess potential for managing people.

60. Exercise: Decide if these questions are behavioural, theoretical /hypothetical, opinion or leading?

- **How would you usually handle difficult people?** Hypothetical - this question is likely to receive a general answer. Ask if the candidate can share a specific example of one individual and talk you through that occasion.

- **Why did you decide to do that?** Opinion - you'll probably receive their opinion. Ask the candidate if they've received any feedback from clients/team members/manager etc.

- **Tell me how you learnt that skill?** Behavioural – it's asking specifically how the candidate went about learning a particular skill. Ensure the candidate doesn't drift into generalising. Watch for words like "tend" or "usually" or "generally"

- **You say their processes were inefficient – how would you change them?** Theoretical or hypothetical – it's likely to get a text book answer. It's asking what would they do and not want they have done. This is okay to understand a candidate's acknowledgement of the situation and learn from their experience.

- **What would your ideal job be?** This is a common / general question which is okay to start the conversation. However, candidates may provide the answer they think you are looking for them to say!

- **Are you a good team player?** Opinion – it's not going to give you much quality evidence of someone's capability or ability – just what they think of themselves.

Behavioural Competencies ~ Quiz Seven Answers

61. Why do we use behavioural competencies to assess candidates during interview?

- Past behaviour is a good predictor of future behaviour
- Excellent tool for gathering job related information
- Excellent tool for assessing a candidate's potential ability to perform in the role
- A useful tool for giving feedback – successful or unsuccessful
- Encourages objective decision making

62. Name at least four different behavioural competencies?

- Planning & Organisation skills
- Communication & Presentation skills
- Time Management skills
- Customer orientation skills

63. What does the acronym S.T.A.R. stand for?

- S = Situation
- T = Task
- A = Actions
- R = Results or outcome

64. Name four key words to watch during the interview?

- Would
- Tend
- Generally
- Usually
- Typically

Planning the Interview ~ Quiz Eight Answers

65. Name at least five things you should consider when planning an interview?

- How many stages in the process?
- Who will be involved in the process?
- How long will each stage take?
- Where are the interviews going to be held?
- Who will be responsible for sending out invitation letters or emails?
- Book the venue or rooms
- Order refreshments or at least have water available
- Print off CVs, Job description, and interview questions
- Inform reception – names of candidates, dates, times and contact name

66. Name at least four different agenda items to cover during a typical interview?

- Introductions
- Explain the interview format / process
- CV background questions & review
- Technical / Job related questions

- Behavioural Competency questions
- General questions – Salary, Notice Period, Holidays, Benefits etc
- Opportunity for the candidate to ask questions
- Explain timings & next steps / stage

67. What could happen if you don't review the CV properly or plan the CV background questions?

- The candidate is likely to take control of the interview
- The candidate will decide what information they will share and it's likely to put them in the best light – it's an interview and they want the job!
- You could lose time "winging it" or thinking up the next question
- You could miss information or gaps on the CV

68. Can you complete the introductions in 120 seconds? Give it a try! I'm part of a Global Networking Organisation and we only have 60 seconds to educate our sales team on our businesses.

Observing & Recording ~ Quiz Nine Answers

69. Give four reasons why taking notes is important?

- Helps the interviewer gather complete examples – Using the STAR process

- It reduces the reliance on memory – Research indicates we only retain 40% of the information after just 3 hours and only 15% after three days!

- Provides data for evaluation at the decision making stage – after interviewing many candidates over a period of time you are likely to forget most of the content if you rely on your memory!

- It reduces the tendency to develop general impressions of the applicant – gathering facts & evidence observed

70. What is "active listening"?

- Active listening is a communication technique which requires the listener to feedback what they hear and understand – the listener is listening to understand not necessarily listening to respond initially.

71. Describe why active listening is important during the interview process?

- Practising active listening will help you build rapport with the candidate and help you focus on understanding the information you are gathering. The typical flow of questions in an interview starts with the open question, this gets the candidate talking then you'll ask a series of probing questions to drill down to the detail. Then you may well paraphrase to check you've understood exactly what the candidate is trying to convey

72. What are you trying not to do during the interview?

- Assess the data or information being gathered or make premature judgements

73. Give four tips on Active Listening?

- Observe the speaker's body language
- Show that you are listening by occasionally nodding & acknowledgements
- Use your own body language and gestures to convey your attention
- Smile and use other facial expressions – some people look very serious when they are trying to concentrate
- Note your posture and make sure it is open and approachable

74. How would you ensure you understood the information being shared during the interview? What techniques would you use?

- Use paraphrasing techniques or reflect back the information to ensure you've understood what the candidate means.

75. If you take lots of notes and don't maintain eye contact what are you in danger of doing?

- Losing rapport with the candidate
- Missing important body language signals

76. For what period of time should you keep notes and records on unsuccessful candidates?

- Best practice would suggest keeping records for unsuccessful candidates for six months. The reason behind this suggestion is that candidates that feel the need to raise a claim of discrimination have three months minus one day after the incident to log the complaint with the Employment Tribunal.

Assessment & Evaluations ~ Quiz Ten Answers

77. What is a Subject Access Request?

- Put simply, the Subject Access Request is section 7 of the Data Protection Act and is normally used by individuals who want to see a copy of information an organisation holds on them

78. Why should you *not* write down your opinion during the interview?

- It's not best practice to judge or assess during the interview and certainly keep un-professional opinions out of note form
- Candidates are entitled to a copy of their interview notes (how would you feel if they read something inappropriate?)
- All records are admissible in court

79. When should you evaluate and assess information gathered on the candidates?

- After the interview is finished – give yourself time to evaluate and reflect on the information gathered and give the candidate proper consideration

80. What percentage of communication is body language?

- 55%

81. What do you need to have with every behavioural competency in order to measure a candidate's competence and future ability?

- Positive & Negative indicators

82. What percentage of communication is the spoken word?

- 7%

83. Explain the horns effect in recruitment terms?

- The "horns" effect lets one negative factor, event or occasion distort the interviewers' decision about that candidate.

84. Explain the halo effect in recruitment terms?

- Conversely the "halo" effect is apparent when the interviewers favour one characteristic or example and let this one positive fact override the entire interview.

Offer Stage & Background Checks ~ Quiz Eleven Answers

85. What are the two main types of offers of employment?

   - Conditional
   - Unconditional

86. Name the two strands of a conditional offer of employment?

   - Either pre-conditional or post conditional

87. How long do you have after someone starts working to issue a written contract?

   - Two months – although, we would recommend a written contract as soon as possible after verbal offer

88. What should be included in a formal offer letter?

   - Job Title & Offer
   - Conditions of Employment (pre-conditions or post-conditions) that apply to the offer – for example, you may wish to state that any Employment Offer is subject to satisfactory

references and background checks, medical examinations (if appropriate for the job or industry), eligibility to work in the UK, or being able to issue certificates of sponsorship or being FCA or PRA registered (if appropriate for the job or industry).

- The terms of the offer - salary, hours, benefits, pension arrangements, holiday entitlement, place of employment, etc
- The date of commencement (start date) and any probationary period
- Outline any actions the candidate needs to take (return a signed acceptance of the offer, agreement to references, any date constraints on acceptance)
- If you intend that the offer letter is to form part of the contract of employment, it should state this fact.

89. What are the minimum requirements by law to include in a contract of employment?

- Name of Employer & Employee
- Job Title & brief description of work
- Start date
- Continuous employment (if the candidate has worked for the same organisation before

within a qualifying period or in a different role)
- Location of work & employers address if different
- Hours of work & Pattern of work (shifts)
- Salary or pay (include benefits) & when you will be paid (weekly, monthly etc.)
- Holiday entitlements
- Notice period for both parties

90. Name the three main background check categories?

- Employment history check
- Document check
- Statutory checks

91. Name four items included in a typical background check?

- Employment history
- Credit history checks
- Criminal records check – Disclosure & Barring Service
- Immigration status

92. What nationalities are automatically eligible to work in the UK?

EU countries are:

- Austria, Belgium, Bulgaria, Croatia, Republic of Cyprus, Czech Republic, Denmark, Estonia, Finland, France, Germany, Greece, Hungary, Ireland, Italy, Latvia, Lithuania, Luxembourg, Malta, Netherlands, Poland, Portugal, Romania, Slovenia, Slovakia, Spain, Sweden and the UK.

European Economic Area (EEA):

- The EEA includes EU countries and also Iceland, Liechtenstein and Norway. It allows them to be part of the EU's single market.

93. Is a verbal offer legally binding contract in the UK?

- Once an "unconditional" job offer has been accepted then it's a legally binding contract – it doesn't have to be in writing or accepted in writing for it to be legally binding.
- If the offer is "conditional" and the candidate is found later not to meet all of the conditions

(reference checks or medical examinations), the offer can be withdrawn by the employer. However, if the candidate meets all the conditions and the offer is later withdrawn it could constitute "breach of contract".

- If the employee accepts an "unconditional" offer and changes their mind – the employer could either make them work their notice or sue for possible "breach of contract".

Induction & On-boarding Process ~ Quiz Twelve Answers

94. What is the Disclosure and Barring Service and what did it replace?

   - The Disclosure and Barring Service (DBS) assists employers to make accurate recruitment decisions and prevent unsuitable people from working with vulnerable groups, including children.
   - It replaces the Criminal Records Bureau (CRB) and Independent Safeguarding Authority (ISA)

95. Name five items to cover with a new joiner on their first day?

   - Meet the team / department
   - Set up equipment – PC, telephone, access cards, ID badges,
   - Tour of the building
   - Health & Safety Orientation
   - HR policies & procedures
   - Sort out payroll details

96. Name at least two items relating to the company orientation and induction?

- Companies History & Senior Management Structure / Organisational Design
- Mission and Vision Statements
- Corporate Values or Principle

97. Name two items relating to the job orientation and induction?

- Job Description – core accountabilities and responsibilities
- Objectives

98. Name two items an employer believes is an implied condition of the psychological contract?

- From the individuals point of view these beliefs could include, a safe working environment, reasonable job security, job satisfaction, promotion, recognition, reward and a flexible approach to work life balance.

99. Name two items an employee believes is an implied condition of the psychological contract?

- From the managers point of view the psychological contract (implied promise or agreement), could include, commitment to achieving set goals and objectives, a sense of loyalty to the business and their colleagues and to achieve a certain level of performance and productivity.

100. What are the possible risks once a candidate has handed in their notice?

- The candidate could be counter offered
- The candidate could continue interviewing with other companies or may even have already committed to attend interviews
- Not turn up on their first day! Sorry to report this has happened!

101. What should you do to mitigate the possible risks once the candidate has handed in their notice?

- Invite to meet the team for coffee or lunch
- Keep in contact – send non-confidential company information to browse or read before their commencement date
- Get the contract signed as soon as possible

About the Author

Dawn Moss and her story: she left school as soon as she could (1984) - well actually it was a bit before the end of the last term!! She wanted to explore life and have fun rather than being stuck in a stuffy and boring class room! With two CSEs to her name she decided she would only be worthy of dead end, low skilled jobs. Her expectations and self esteem were set pretty low and that good old prophecy (that's the self fulfilling one!), gave her the results she expected and believed she deserved.

She mainly worked in shops and cleaned for a living. Don't get the wrong idea – she loved those jobs at the time and worked very hard, she was loyal, punctual and diligent (a few words there she wouldn't have even been able to spell back then!).

Dawn has since gained a 2:1 Honours Degree in Health Promotion (1995), qualified as a Human Resource Professional and gained Membership to the Chartered Institute of Personnel Development (2007). She has trained with SHL the leaders in Psychometrics and can administer and interpret psychometric ability tests and personality questionnaires. She has trained as a Personal and Career Coach and is a member of the Association of Coaching (2010).

Dawn has worked in a corporate blue chip environment for over a decade and now runs a coaching and training practice.

She has coached and interviewed hundreds if not thousands of people during her career in Human Resources and as a Life & Career Coach and now wants to share what she believes to be vital and valuable information on interview skills for hiring managers.

Thank you for purchasing the prerequisite to her Interview Guide & Tool Kit. Enjoy learning and good luck in the next interview!!

Don't forget that we are here to help you with your recruitment questions – and we provide a 'done for you service' too!

To get in touch, simply visit http://www.yourinterviewcoach.co.uk or call 07932 434 303

About the book & toolkit

Interview Guide for Busy Managers

How to Select the Best Talent!

For details of the full Interview Guide book go to:

http://www.yourinterviewcoach.co.uk

How the book is structured

We have organised the guide in the same logical process as the recruitment process itself. Each chapter is dedicated to a part of the recruitment process. There's an introduction to the subject and then we go on to give you lots of options, examples, case studies and some anecdotes to boot!

We have written this guide to bring together all the information, templates and examples you'll need to design your own recruitment process to suit your business requirements. Or at least get you on the right track!

Chapter One gives you an overview of the entire **Recruitment Process** where we'll discuss the most important factors to consider for an effective process of getting the right person with the right skills and some common problems and how to overcome them.

Chapter Two is all about giving you an easy understanding of the legal framework which will hopefully help you in **Getting to Know UK Employment Law.** Employment law is complex and this manual cuts through the bureaucratic nature of legislation and gets directly to the dos and don'ts!

It's important that you understand the legal framework before you get started on sourcing and selecting people for your business. We'll share lots of practical examples and the case law – to give some insight and context to the definitions and descriptions.

Chapter Three helps you to get really clear about the requirements for the job and about the person you are ideally seeking to be able to conduct and create the **Job Analysis & Job Description.**

We'll give you plenty of options to analyse the different jobs in your organisation and key elements to include in the Job Description & Person Specification. There's also a couple of templates you can use, amend or brand as you wish.

Chapter Four is all about finding the most appropriate and relevant people by using various **Sourcing Methods – Attracting & Finding People.** We'll give you lots of different options for attracting and sourcing the right and most appropriate person to fit your job and business.

There is particular attention to Social Media – most of the platforms are free and if you're not currently using these platforms you are most certainly behind

the curve. Stop burying your head in the sand –
Social Media is not going away any time soon!

Chapter Five is concerned with the techniques you
use to assess a person's skills and knowledge with
Selection Methods – Assessing People.

Using the right tools for your business and the job
requirements is so important. We'll talk about the
validity and reliability of different selection methods.

Chapter Six is designed to inform you about the
various **Questioning Techniques** available and
what are the most effective in job interviews.
Asking the right questions is absolutely essential to
get the right information – sounds easy yes?! You'll
be surprised how many managers ask their set of
favourite questions time and time again and don't
actually get the real evidence they need to make a
good decision.

What is it that you are trying to do in the interview?
You are trying to predict the future potential,
behaviour and capability of that candidate. Asking
general, closed or hypothetical questions only
gathers someone's knowledge of a subject – not
their behavioural competence.

Chapter Seven is all about the most useful and effective tool you can have in your interview skill set; the **Behavioural Competency Questions**. Successfully predicting a candidate's behaviour is one of the most important sections of this book. I'm a big advocate of using behavioural competency style interview questions and have thousands of examples of applying this technique with successful outcomes.

There have been many arguments and debates over the years whether interviewing is an Art or a Science! The answer is "Yes it is!"

Chapter Eight is about making good use of your time during the interview by properly **Planning the Interview.** You've heard the old cliché "Fail to plan, plan to fail". Well it's very relevant to the interview process.

You'll be surprised how quickly time will fly in the interview itself and there are plenty of time bandits – we'll show you how to avoid these common mistakes.

Chapter Nine will help you to be methodical in **Observation & Recording Information.** Demonstrating how you made a decision on a candidate's suitability is essential in these litigious times and part of proving how you've made a decision requires supporting documentation.

How should you write interview notes? How long should you keep the interview notes and records on candidates? Chapter Nine will explain.

Chapter Ten explains the process after the interview; **Evaluation & Assessment** of the data and information you have gathered during the interview stage.

We'll show you how the techniques you can apply during the interview stage to gather information can now be used to assess and evaluate that information.

Chapter Eleven is all about that all important **Offer Stage.** It's a great feeling getting to the end of the recruitment process and identifying the person you would like to join the team. It's essential that you've managed expectations properly throughout the entire process for this stage to go smoothly.

Some key factors to consider are shared in this chapter. There have been some significant changes to background referencing recently and no doubt will be an area subjected to more change and shake up in the future.

Chapter Twelve explains how to get off on the right foot before someone joins the company by properly considering the **Induction and On-boarding** process. The person's psychological contract started way before the first day in their new job, so it's important that everyone involved in the recruitment process has managed expectations realistically.

There should be a warm welcome to the company to ensure that the employment relationship gets off on the right foot!

What's in the Tool Kit?

This section will reference the additional material and templates available to use AS IS or brand to your business.

We wanted this book to go beyond providing guidance and instructions. We wanted to provide small to medium businesses with a range of templates that can be rebranded and reference material to help put the information into context.

In this age of technology it's easy to find information on the web but have you ever spent all day on the internet and actually achieved nothing?

It's a bit like years ago when we would use a dictionary – we'd probably end up looking up 3 more words.

It's like that when you start an internet search – you get carried away clicking on all the links that take you down a completely different theme to the one you started your search!   Next thing you know it is hours later....oops!

This toolkit has done all the hard work and searching for you and bought it all into one place. It's taken me 12 years and 4 months to write this toolkit! (But worth the wait I'm sure you'll agree!).

Tool Kit & Appendix

- UK Employment Law – Seven Employment Tribunal Case Studies

- Job Description Template (Available on-line)

- Application Form Template (Available on-line)

- CV Screening Template – Word (Available on-line)

- CV Screening Template – Excel (Available on-line)

- Blank Interview Questions Template (Appendix & Available on-line)

- 100 Behavioural Competency Questions (Covering 17 different Competencies, Motivational Questions and questions typically asked by candidates). (Appendix)

- Behavioural Competencies & Positive & Negative Indictors – Examples (Appendix)

- Scoring & Rating Templates – Word (Available on-line)

- Scoring & Rating Templates – Excel (Available on-line)

- Reference Request Letter – Template (Appendix & Available on-line)

- Induction Checklist – First Day, First Week & First Month (Appendix & Available on-line)

- Health & Safety Orientation Checklist (Appendix & Available on-line)

- Fire Instructions & Evacuation Procedure (Appendix & Available on-line)

Thank you for completing the Quiz!
We hope you enjoyed it.

Dawn Moss MCIPD

www.ingramcontent.com/pod-product-compliance
Lightning Source LLC
Chambersburg PA
CBHW051710170526
45167CB00002B/607